WHITE DOE

WHITE DOE

MARIA WILLIAMS

SADDLE ROAD PRESS

White Doe © Maria Williams 2024

Saddle Road Press
Ithaca, New York
saddleroadpress.com

Book design and frontcover image by Don Mitchell
Back cover image by Larassa Kabel
Author photo by Lyric Williams-Russell

ISBN 9798987954171
Library of Congress Control Number: 2024932668

For my dad

Peter Charles Williams

Contents

I

I

THE DOE

weather—
on the other side of the glass
a meat truck pushes through it on the road

thick flakes stick to telephone wires

would you like a cup of coffee?
milk, you say, a bowl

white doe like glass
white doe among the evergreens
white doe beside the shed beside the house
white doe under the covers, hooves sticking out

we sit sipping beside the window
put dishes in the sink, sigh
over the lip of the drain

I am alone, dad, I am in mourn and
quiet, between us

a small chorus of trees

you start crying like the birds
you were crying yesterday

there the common room
this the apostrophe

✻

in which hand do I hold
the feathers?
what heart the string?

it is not enough to witness
you forgetting

coyotes, dad, coyotes

here is a red coat and a pocketful of seed
here are two sticks for making fire

I wish I could give you antlers
or sharper teeth

        crusted top
        crystal loam
        angry wind snow

how will I know you are with me?

north, you say
you lean over the lip of it, north

✺

do you remember my name?

yes, but it's hiding
your name is my name hiding

white doe alone
white doe crossing the rabbit tracks
white disappears in the clouds

who are we now? you shout toward the window

✳

1. let's count the hoof prints in the snow
2. the fire
3. I will go foraging and you will throw seed
4. your hands a small steeple

what about the people with the pistols?
you cry, no

I say, ghost

we hear a crack in the field, birds rush
from their branches

5. grab the hymnal!
6. the bowl!

I bought you a coat
I wrote your name in the lining

❁

there goes a rabbit under a bush!

and the urge to crack
        its skull and drink

the house, its windows out
slow churning of the cistern

I am pretending
to be a wolf—you a fish
almost dead and out of water

our snowsuits chafe the sky

the geese have gone worry, you say
your nose drips

white doe
her family
white her glass eye

dad, I'm hungry
        a rabbit is everything and there it goes

❀

quiet

      and a deer
treads outside our window

this small church

      like when I read Aygi
peering over the edge of each letter

into the dark folds
          of a drift

❋

I turn on the light

outside
the glowing windows say

     here is your salvation
to whomever

        passes

we reach out our hands
over the dull edge of Formica

     the bruised skin of milk

soon
the child in each of us will be
fully wept

you begin to sing
     bring me back as a small bird

✳

then you look at me
the way you look through

      snow, as if I could

walk into the storm
disappear

✽

morning—
the electricity's out
what's in the field?
what's in the ever-folding snow mounds?

a plow scrapes the street
smoke rises into sky

why are the birds here?
why don't they fly?

✳

dad, look! feathers
glistening in the drive—the doe

her carpet unrolled
squirrels and other creatures in the yard

you run for your slippers, say, milk, but
we're out

say, the corncobs are in the garage

I want you to wait
want to say coat

but the heaters are hissing a procession
begun

coffee?
no

white doe comes and nuzzles your cheek
white her wet nose
white and you laughing

II

BOAT

if dementia were a boat
it would be

     the moon

if a moon, a submarine

no particular

orbit
perpetual

      night

her flying objects

space trash
black flies

         a child

paddling without a sea

his mother
     whose mother
         lady in the ink

no one to whisper get up its late time for bed

it's good
to see you

       moon

come sit by the porthole
wipe your spoon

    enjoy a parade of

    muzac

soft

    foods

barbed

    sleep

dementia would be

a man

      floating past
a spaceship window

             a cow

with its head caught in

the lake

my father essaying through a field
against

frozen stalks of rain

      a property change
the air into

        atmosphere

shit on the wall

he keeps putting his hands in his pants and smearing
feces on the flowered paper

to hieroglyphs

a new language
from

a black cave

bats batsb atsbats mba tsbats

fly out his mouth by the thousands

My Father as Bird

staring at the small intestine of the brain
in the doctor's office—

hello amygdala
right hemisphere
hello—

a hummingbird comes to me

little bird
I say

he peels my hand off the vinyl upholstery

everything I know is
wind

wings

and now the doctor says, I can't exactly
calculate progress or decline

sliced into seventy beats per second

like the thrum
                of a string

even the light is flayed into tiny shards of light

My Father as Coyote

the moon
ribbons the snow blue

       and that makes me

not what you think

four paws
four toes each

this is how we are

     everything, even

here in the dark

    breath

      smokestacks

this is how
   we

      are

      everything
  even
    here

A Man Has Been Found Dead

I

we make fires, mom and I
encircle the house with stones

she keeps calling it dreamland
we are in dreamland, young one

all these prayers long arrows of milk

ironing board, she instructs
coffee cups from the sill

as if this were a summer house

sheets come out, vague
shapes of chairs

who are we now? I ask as she smooths
the outline of a body from the bed

go throw salt in arcs over the yard

I hope the birds don't mistake salt for seed

II

where have you been?

his jacket leaks feather
his gloves have sunk over his hands

would you like a cup of coffee?

by the door
by the bay window

stalactites of ice

words disappeared in drifts

he is a leaky faucet, a bad omen
he is just moccasins!

his
purple hands
twitch

underneath the snow is a door, I whisper

III

everything is an argument
against the pursuant cold

he is not gone, I plead

she puts my photo in a box and
wraps the cord

in the back room, his legs are
two gleaming tusks

eyes like shining icicles from the roof

is that what we call the soul?

the sun is setting
in the doorway, she darkens too

as if *to be* is a place *to go*

IV

when I am old, these fires will be
nothing but soot

salt will rim my bones
not that I wish for it

he sleeps a lot now

for example, the wash
for example, the door still open
for example, ice on the trees

who are we now? he questions the ceiling

I climb onto his chest
          and press my ear to it

SQUALL

what wind
picks up the snow and skates it
                              over the white fields?

what factory? how many black trees?

in the distance
           wires meet

                  an inch
balances on the branches

soon come the coyotes
their thick coats

how many accidents? how many
                        bleating in the air?

III

SNOW

there

                                         are

                                 two kinds

of people

                                                       birds

                                                     and

                                                coyotes

so

a pocketful

of seed

is equal

to a

smattering

of feathers

be
careful

where

you

step

word

travels

as song

as

scent

roads

end

an

old

coyote

once

said

as

he

pulled

at

his

chest

flesh

is only

part

of

    the

hunt

if

I was

a

fiercer

daughter

made

with

wings

                                        if it

                        was

                        not

        death

        but

                thought

the

                                                     sky   is

                   big

                                                        white

a crane

                                        sounds

                         in

                                the

                         distance

see

the

wind

against

his

body

each step

is a door

hinge

a joint

    swing

the red

       against

       white

           is not

    a cardinal

a body

        says

          take me

          as I am

                 then

          talking

          ends

small

      birds

         carry

                small

notes

         of

               twig

hands

                   feet

         eyelash

bring

me

back

a

bird

for

my

window

I

scream

breath

leaks

past

my cheeks

as

we

are

now

is

the

way

snow

is

IV

SEABED

there is a man whose job is to lead me through the mortuary
to lay his hand over the knob of my shoulder and weigh me down

fluorescents flicker, a steel table shines
under dad's arching spine

take your time, the man says, and I wonder how
many nights I'll have to stay here, how many years

there is the body, empty, the scar
of the man's palm on my shoulder

and the light, green and rakish
through which I watch him turn and walk away

✻

shall I kneel on the floor, dad
and raise my eyes to that light?

Burying the Dog

we carried her body as one
carries a human body

placed it in the car, drove slowly
over blackbirds, cowbirds, grackles

we carried her up a long slope, clumsily
almost unable to reach the hole

it was late, the two of us
shivering

we lifted her in an old blue blanket
two corners each, our silhouettes folding and refolding

if memory meant love
we left her, the maggots knitting

her skin by early evening
clicking their sticks, they ate and ate

then we drove back over the birds as people do
to spend the night in our beds

WALK-THROUGH

the cups are gone
that missing   painting on the wall

shines its own sun like dirt

there is the chair he'd been
heavy in for days

                its back ribs bowing

a house is a chair
that holds

our weight

      a heart that breaks its own
          caning

mom says she'll kill me if I come near

    she would
send letters if she knew how

                to write

    the body too
        is an animal

        a small vase
that brass plate someone earned somewhere in a war

I remember mom

     burying herself
        in dead leaves on the lawn

days before she spoke and then
the way a chain   saws

someone is feeding all your missing
things into the furnace

      the house says

          someone is expecting

I pretend not to hear it   the mind
is a creature I can't believe

     we had a dog once   maggots
wove a rug of its skin

the problem is being   porous
and the house is

     covered in its own membrane

where I've slipped   in

     I am rearranging
all the furniture in my mind

      there is no furniture, but   I am moving it

the sill
covered in coffee rings and flies

the dog   nobody loved it

the vet said she had worms all through   like a piece of wood

with which hand do I hold the dead?
the house never answers

with what shovel, what cup?

MY FATHER AS CARCASS, MY MOTHER AS FLY

see how she hovers
over that terrified hole—his mouth

a blazing window as if all questions are
answered by a great blast of sun

see his ribs stretched white and her wet
wings shimmering, eyes

multiplying the many years
this must be love—

how she touches down on his lips
and nibbles there

how she lights on his chin and rubs
her tiny hands to start a tiny fire

maybe her heart is in those hands
as it has always been—busy, burning

I admit it is good
to see her weightless

finally, winged, forgetting all
I have not forgiven yet

hi, mom—
I whisper into the tomb

see her pause then alight, land
on his eye and pierce

the smallest pinpricks
into his cornea

see the sun's dark
crown

you are both still inside me, she whispers back
this the end and the beginning

his palms are small cups, come and drink

V

How I Pray

north

❃

a length of string thrown
to a waving field of white

＊

package of seed

here

      a cup of coffee

 here of milk

✻

I place your picture on the sill

✺

flock of geese

❀

who are we now who are we now who are we

FUNERAL

when the pope died and the funeral was on

a cardinal hopped from the feeder to the bush back
to the feeder

I was too young to know how to be
alive

the red bird flitted to a tree, it disappeared
amid the branching

I turned from the window back
to the room, that womb

to find dad weeping at the set

so strange
to have heard his grief as wingbeat

Don't Be Afraid

word of your passing has reached the tree line

now the animals
sing

mom and I sing too
from our spines—those reedy hollows

❋

crocuses pierce the earth beside the house
as if

we were not alone
all winter

what else is *to be*
but light? we sing

what else to be but light

❋

in which I can almost see you
glistening

you would love it the music rising

❋

there are questions without answers
love and its mistakes

don't be afraid
the animals sing

in darkness
we all open our palms

❋

form constellations

❋

find the
        paw prints
                in the snow

ACKNOWLEDGMENTS

Thank you to *Quarterly West, Pank, Allium,* and *Grey Suit Editions Online* for publishing early and current sections of this book and to the Vermont Studio Center, A Room of One's Own Foundation, Vermont College of the Arts, and the Summer Literary Seminars for giving me time, inspiration, and space to write.

Much thanks to Maggie Smith and Marcela Sulak whose keen skills helped fine-tune this work, and to my poet friends who read and critiqued multiple versions of these poems. Gratitude to books from Gennady Aygi, Michael Dickman, and Jean Valentine, which sat close to me for much of the writing of this book.

White Doe is the winner of the Verse Daily Prize, chosen by JP Dancing Bear, and a proud semifinalist for the Perugia Prize, The Wisconsin Poetry Series Bittingham and Felix Pollak Poetry Prize from the University of Wisconsin Press, The Washington Prize from Word Works, and The Wilder Prize from Two Sylvias Press.

About the Author

Maria Williams is the author of the chapbook *A Love Letter To Say There Is No Love* (FutureCycle Press, 2011). A Pushcart Prize nominee, she is also the recipient of residencies and fellowships from Jentel, Pen America, and the Vermont Studio Center,

among others. Her poems have been published in numerous journals including *Bellevue Literary Review*, *Pank*, and *Quarterly West*.

An adoptee and mother to Maya and Lyric, two artists in their own right, Maria's work centers around themes of belonging, abandonment, family, and relationships. She lives and writes in the Pioneer Valley of western Massachusetts.